I0804429

MEGA BOOKS

MACHINES

CHRISTIANE GUNZI

Gareth Stevens PUBLISHING

**Please visit our website,
www.garethstevens.com.
For a free color catalog of all
our high-quality books, call
toll free 1-800-542-2595 or
fax 1-877-542-2596.**

Published in 2025 by
Gareth Stevens Publishing
2544 Clinton St.
Buffalo, NY 14224

Copyright © Picthall and Gunzi, an imprint of Award Publications Limited

Written and edited by: Christiane Gunzi
Designer: Paul Calver
Editorial assistant: Maudie Gunzi
Heavy machinery consultant: Gary Boyd-Hope

Picthall & Gunzi would particularly like to thank the following companies for the use of their images:
Bucyrus International, Inc.; Caterpillar Inc.; Komatsu Ltd.; Liebherr (manufacturer of the world's largest cranes); Nathan Kress from Kress Corporation; Terex; Tesmec USA, Inc.

Cataloging-in-Publication Data

Names: Gunzi, Christiane.
Title: Machines / Christiane Gunzi.
Description: Buffalo, NY : Gareth Stevens Publishing, 2025. | Series: Mega books
Identifiers: ISBN 9781482467994 (pbk.) | ISBN 9781482468007 (library bound) | ISBN 9781482468014 (ebook
Subjects: LCSH: Machinery--Juvenile literature. | Mechanical engineering--Juvenile literature. | Engineering--Juvenile literature.
Classification: LCC TJ147.G86 2025 | DDC 621.8--dc23

All rights reserved. No part of this book may be reproduced in any form without
permission in writing from the publisher, except by a reviewer.

Printed in the United States of America

CPSIA compliance information: Batch #CSGS25: For further information contact Gareth Stevens at 1-800-542-2595.

Find us on

CONTENTS

GIANT EXCAVATORS

This is the biggest excavator in the world. It has a bucket at the front that is as big as a bus. The excavator is very tough so it can travel over rocks. The driver's cab is so big that there is also space for a computer, a fridge, and a microwave!

Can you see some steps?

Mega load

This excavator is loading up one of the world's biggest dump trucks. It can load tons of earth and rocks very quickly.

Wow!

See how tiny these chidren are next to the big excavator!

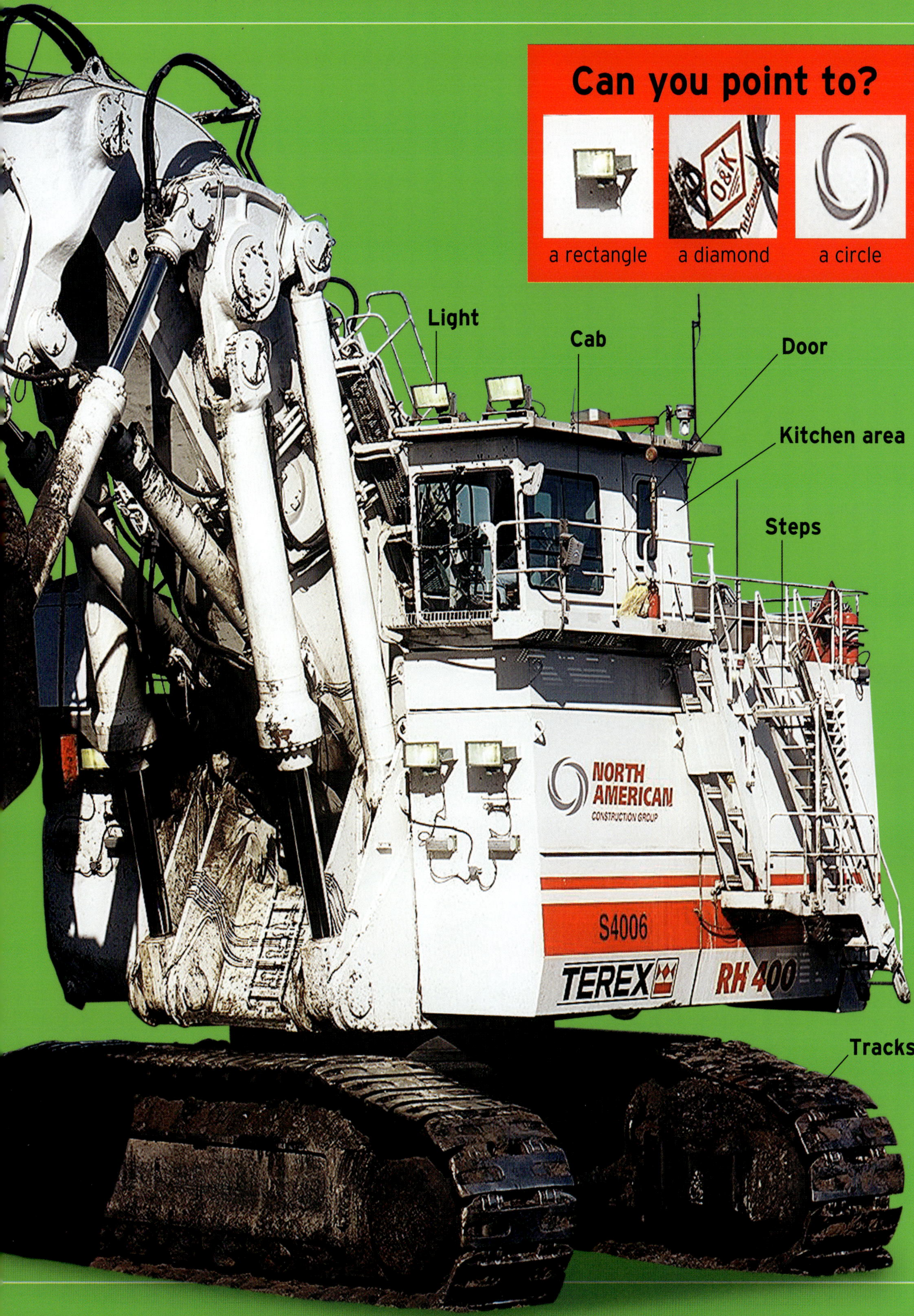

Can you point to?

a rectangle

a diamond

a circle

SCRAPERS

Machines called scrapers cut the top layer off the ground. They make it flat so that roads can be put on top. Scrapers need lots of power so they have two huge engines, one at the front and one at the back!

Can you point to?

a number

an air filter

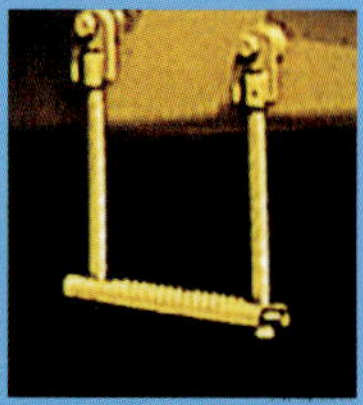

a step

How many engines does a scraper have?

Here, two scrapers are working together to make a new road.

Big bowl

As the machine scrapes the ground, it collects earth in the bowl. When the bowl is full, the driver empties the earth out through the bottom and starts all over again.

ROCK SAWS

This amazing machine is the world's biggest rock saw. It has a huge wheel at the front with teeth that can cut through solid rock. There are two stabilizers to keep the saw steady.

Sharp teeth

The driver can make the wheel turn quickly or slowly. All around the wheel there are steel cutting teeth that saw into the ground as the wheel turns.

What job does this mega machine do?

Tracks

The rock saw crawls along on tracks. The driver controls the cutting wheel from a seat in the cab at the back of the machine.

SLAB CARRIERS

These machines carry big, heavy slabs of steel around the factory. Carriers are really strong. They move quickly and can load and unload themselves.

Can you point to?

some lights

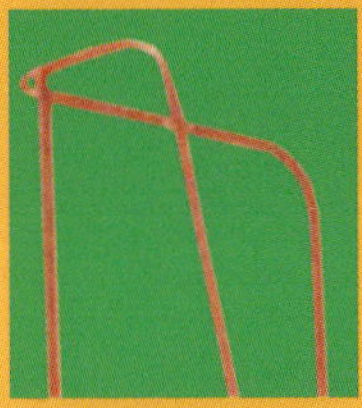

a safety rail

some steps

Super steering

The cab has two steering wheels and the seat turns all the way around so the driver can drive forward or backward.

Straddle carrier

This machine is called a straddle carrier. It can pick up red-hot slabs of steel. The straddle carrier moves very fast. It has good brakes so it can stop quickly too.

A straddle carrier picking up steel slabs

What do these machines carry?

LADLE CARRIERS

Ladle carriers are used in steelworks. They pick up, carry, and dump huge, heavy buckets. The buckets are called ladles, or slag pots. They carry hot liquid metal and ash. Each machine has big tires to help it carry its load.

Melting metal

This ladle carrier is tipping out a pot full of boiling-hot metal. It looks like the lava in a volcano!

Where is the big slag pot?

Cozy cab

These machines load and unload themselves so the driver can stay in the cab.

Mega load

These carriers have big tires like the ones on an aircraft. They can carry 550 tons (500 mt)!

MINING SHOVELS

Massive mining shovels like this one work in coal mines and quarries. They crawl along on their huge, wide tracks. Strong steel ropes pull the big bucket up and down as it picks up earth and moves it to another place.

All around

This amazing mining shovel can turn all the way around. It has a huge cab so that the driver can work easily.

Big bucket

This machine works quickly and it can hold 110 tons (100 mt) of earth in its bucket.

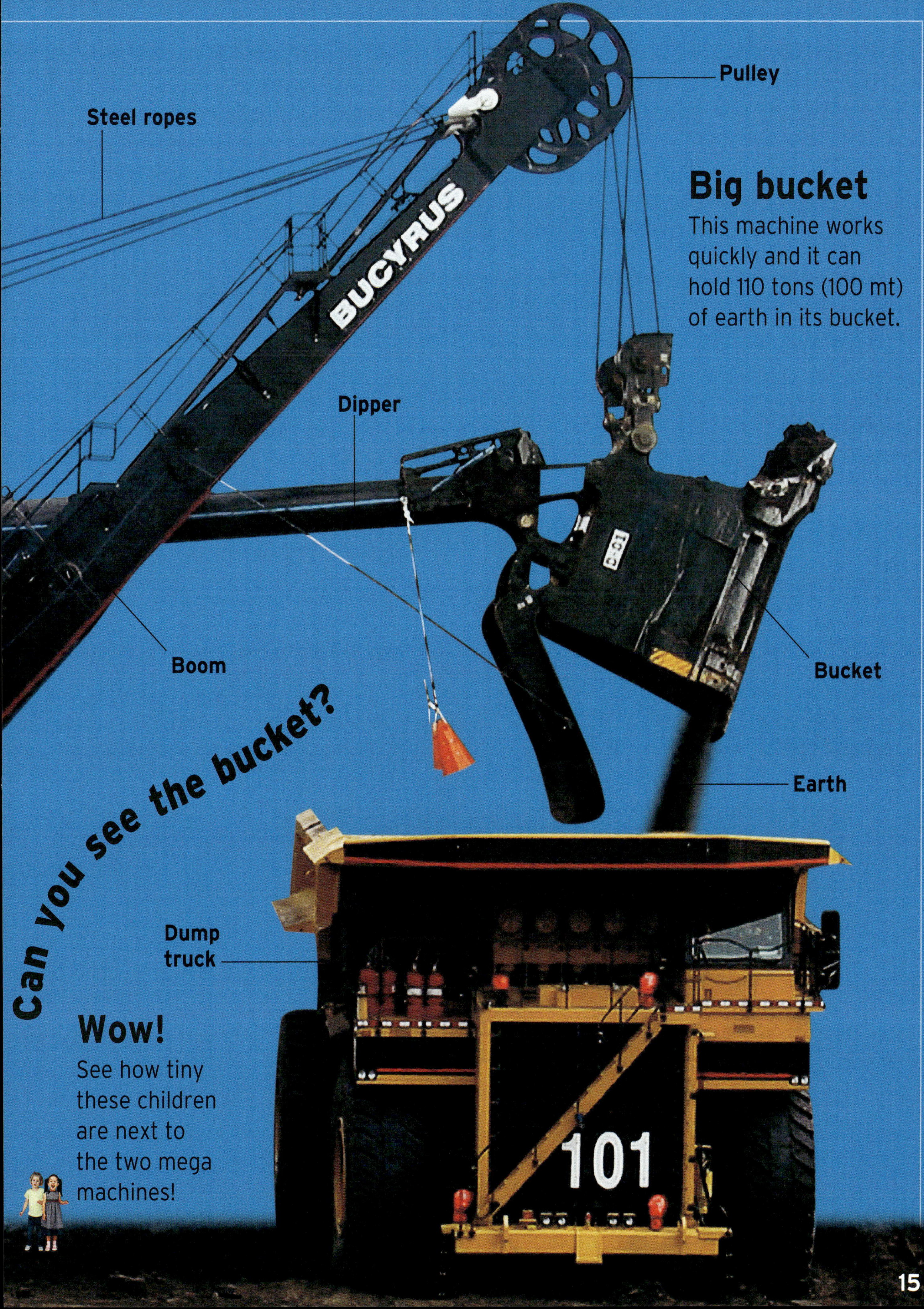

Can you see the bucket?

Wow!

See how tiny these children are next to the two mega machines!

BLASTHOLE DRILLS

This huge drill is used for drilling holes in quarries. The tall mast carries big rods that can drill a very long way into the ground. When the hole is deep enough, explosives are put inside. They explode and blow big chunks of rock out of the ground, ready to be collected.

Mega mast

Blasthole drills usually move along on tracks. But sometimes they are carried on trailers that have lots of wheels. When the drill is being moved from one place to another, the mast has to lay down flat.

Can you see a hook at the top of the mast?

Can you point to?

a cross | two rectangles | a circle | little squares

COLD PLANERS

A cold planer is a special machine used for building roads and motorways. As it drives along it takes off all the old concrete and asphalt. This machine has four motors and they can work at two different speeds.

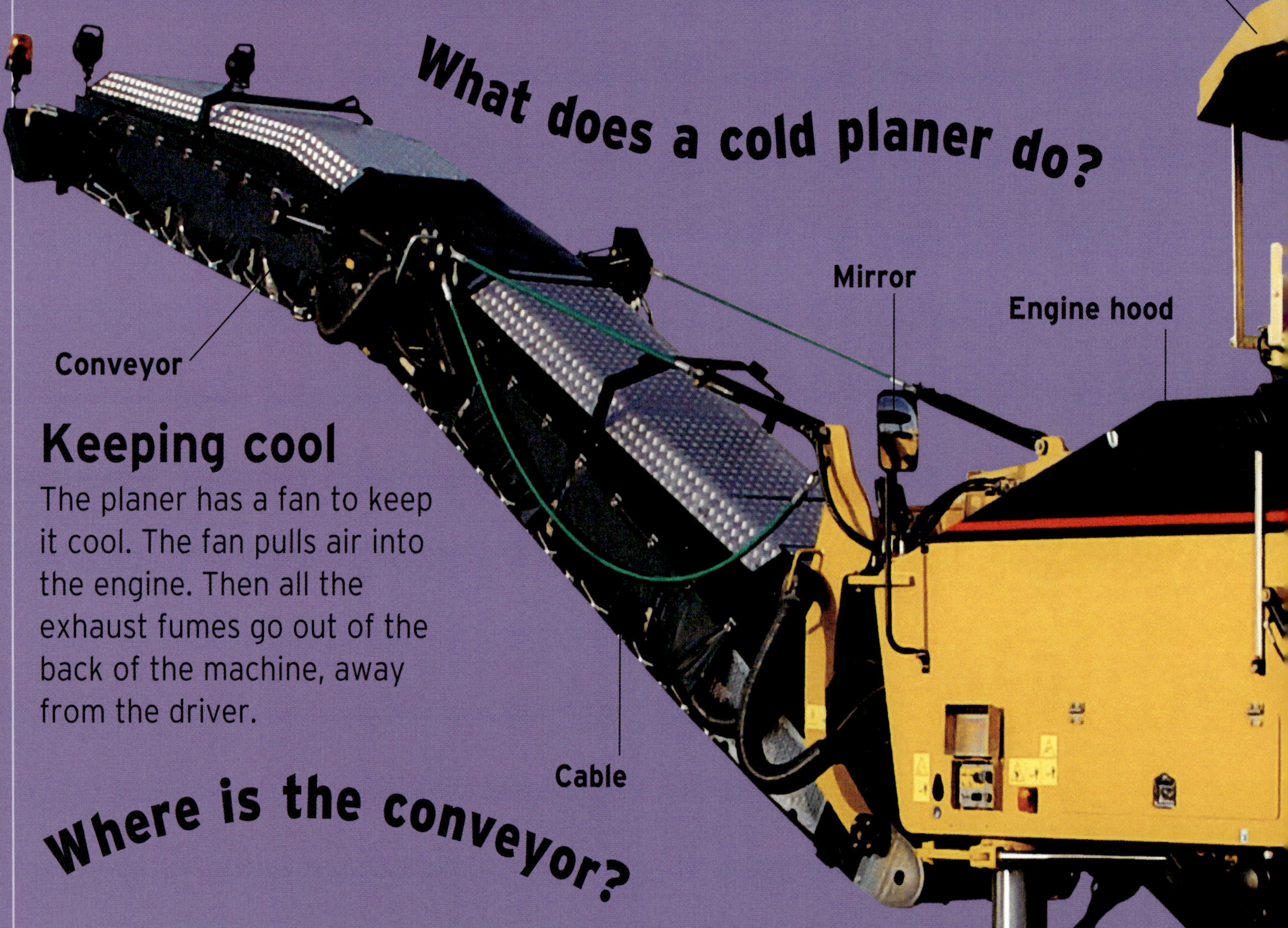

What does a cold planer do?

Keeping cool

The planer has a fan to keep it cool. The fan pulls air into the engine. Then all the exhaust fumes go out of the back of the machine, away from the driver.

Where is the conveyor?

Can you point to?

some chevrons

a light

some letters

Clever conveyor

The long part on the front of the planer is called the conveyor. The rubble shoots out of the end and into a truck. When the job is finished, the driver can fold the conveyor in half.

HUGE HAULERS

Haulers are used in coal mining. They carry coal from the mine to the place where it is stored. This big hauler has eight huge wheels to help it carry the weight. The driver dumps the coal out of the bottom of the truck. A canopy over the cab protects the driver in case any of the coal falls out.

Wow!

Can you see the two boys? They are three years old. See how tiny they are next to the mega hauler!

As big as a house

Haulers have to be enormous so that they can carry masses of coal. Some haulers are so big that you could fit a house inside their dump body!

How many wheels does this hauler have?

SUPER DOZERS

The super dozer is one of the most powerful bulldozers in the world. It is so massive that when it is carried on a truck it has to be taken in lots of pieces.

Can you point to?

a number | some tracks | some cables

How many lights can you see on this machine?

Mega blade

The driver controls the super dozer's massive blade from inside the cab. The blade can push, dig, carry, and dump huge loads of earth and rocks.

Wow!

This little girl is three years old. See how tiny she is next to the super dozer!

DRAGLINES

This gigantic machine is called a dragline. It is used for getting earth and rock out of coal mines so that the coal can be dug out. A big bucket hangs off the front of the machine. The dragline swings out and drops the bucket. Then steel ropes drag the bucket along the ground and back up, filling it with earth on the way.

Super steel

Draglines need strong steel ropes so that they can work properly. These ropes connect to rope winders inside the machine. The winders are called drums. The driver controls the drums from inside the cab.

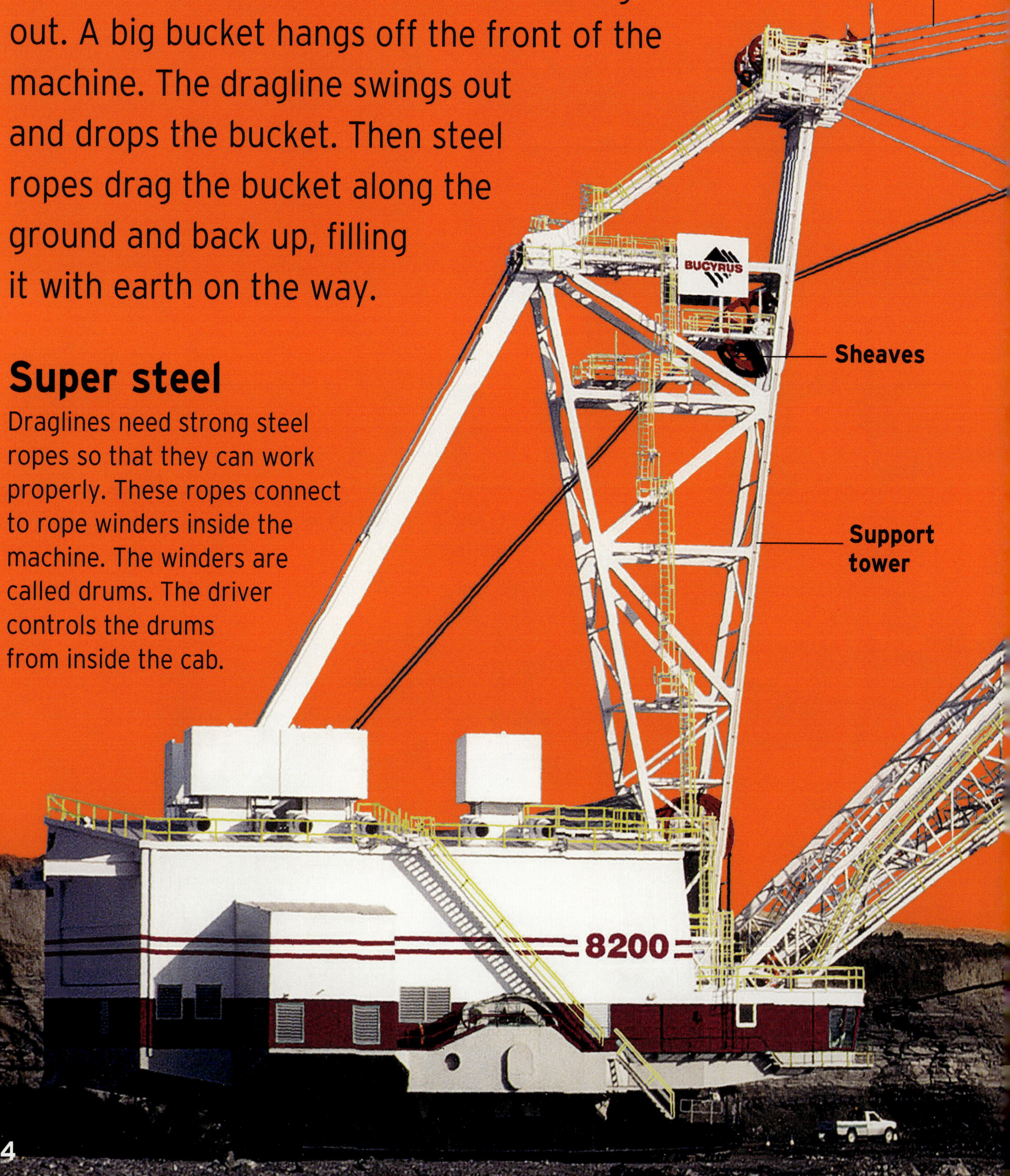

Where is the drag bucket?

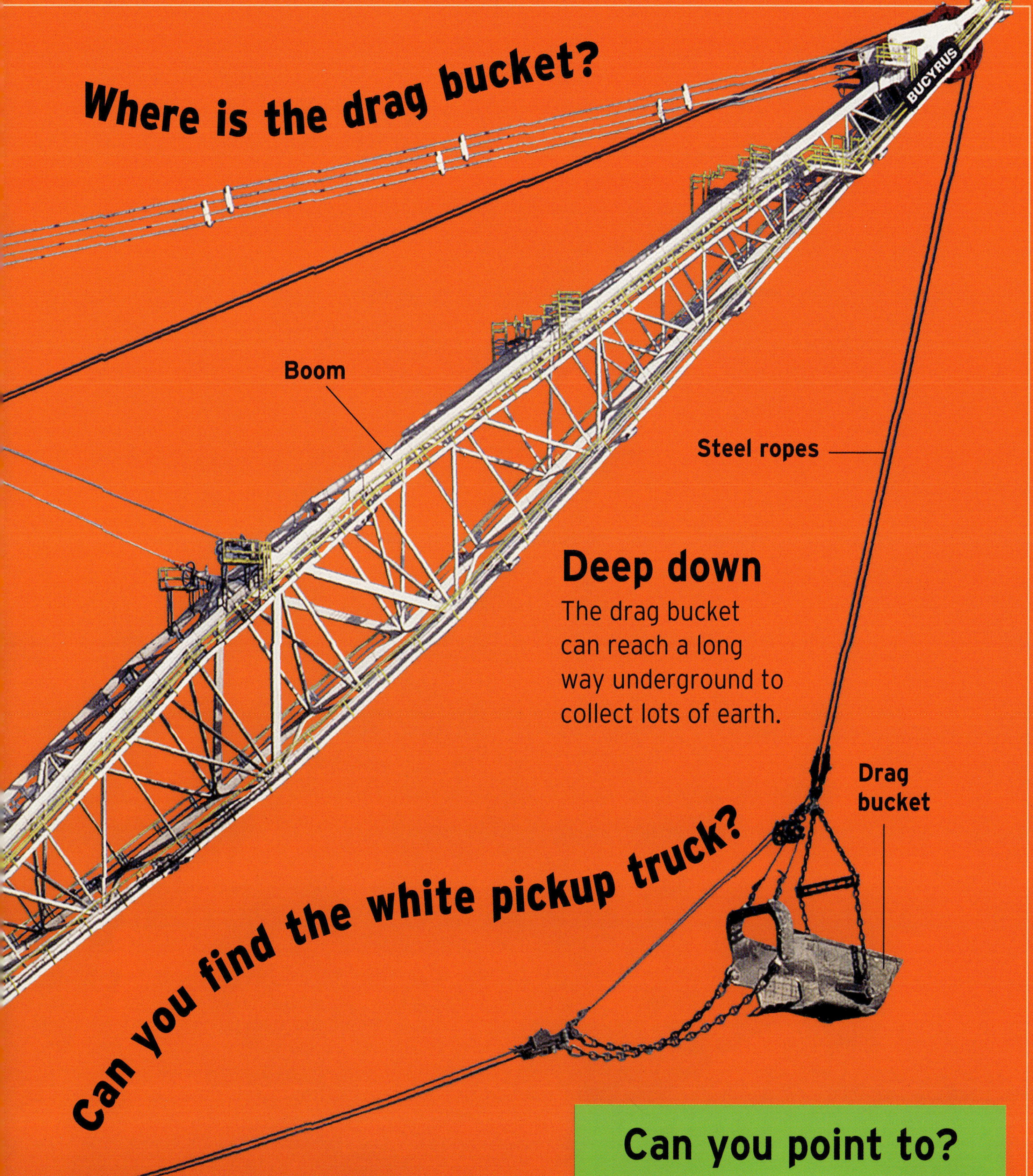

Deep down

The drag bucket can reach a long way underground to collect lots of earth.

Can you find the white pickup truck?

Can you point to?

a triangle

two stripes

some squares

TRENCHERS

A trencher is used for digging long, thin trenches in hard ground. It has a gigantic chainsaw on the front. All the rubble is carried along on a conveyor belt and shoots out of the back.

Can you point to?

some lights

a piston

a chainsaw

Mega chainsaw

At the front of the trencher there is a long chainsaw. It is very strong. Trenchers work in the same way as the chainsaws that are used for cutting down trees.

What do you think the stabilizers are for?

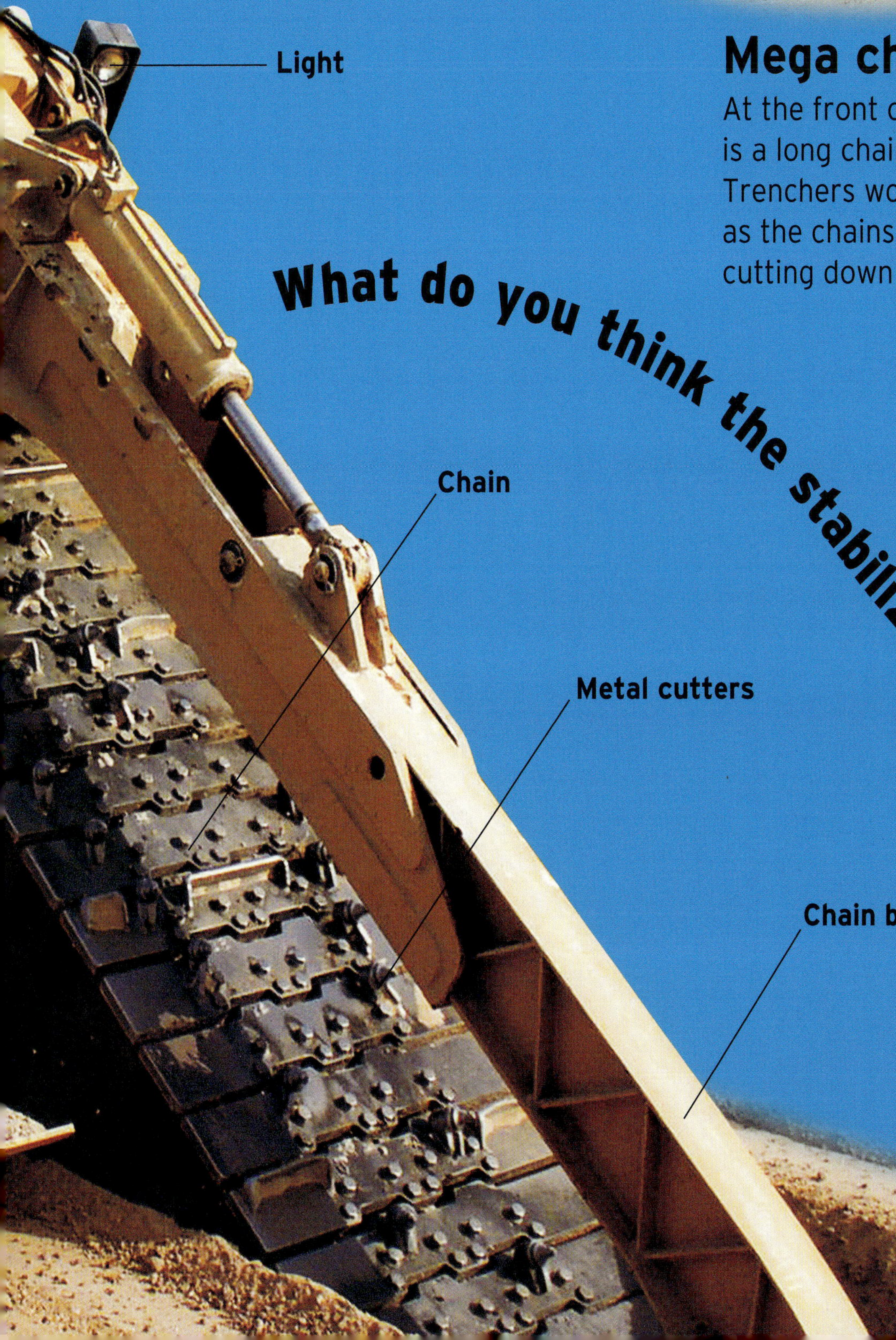

PIPE LAYERS

Special machines called pipe layers are used for putting long pipes into the ground. The pipes are so heavy that each machine has to have an extra weight on the opposite side to help it to balance.

Standing tall

When a pipe layer moves along on its tracks, the crane jib has to stay upright to help the machine balance.

How many machines can you see?

Busy tractors

All these tractors are carrying one long, heavy oil pipe. They each have a crane jib attached on one side to help them to carry the pipe.

Up high

The machine is high above the ground so it cannot get stuck in the mud as it drives along on its wide tracks.

Can you point to?
some chevrons
an exhaust
a pulley
Pulley
Steel wire
Crane jib
Exhaust pipe
Air filter
Tracks

GIANT CRANES

Tall cranes are used on building sites and in harbors for loading and unloading ships. This huge crane can lift 1,100 tons (1,000 mt), which is like picking up 125 double-decker buses. At the back there are weights to stop it from falling over when it is lifting. The crane can lift things high up into the air.

Grab it

This crane has a special part called a grab for moving sand, rock, and coal.

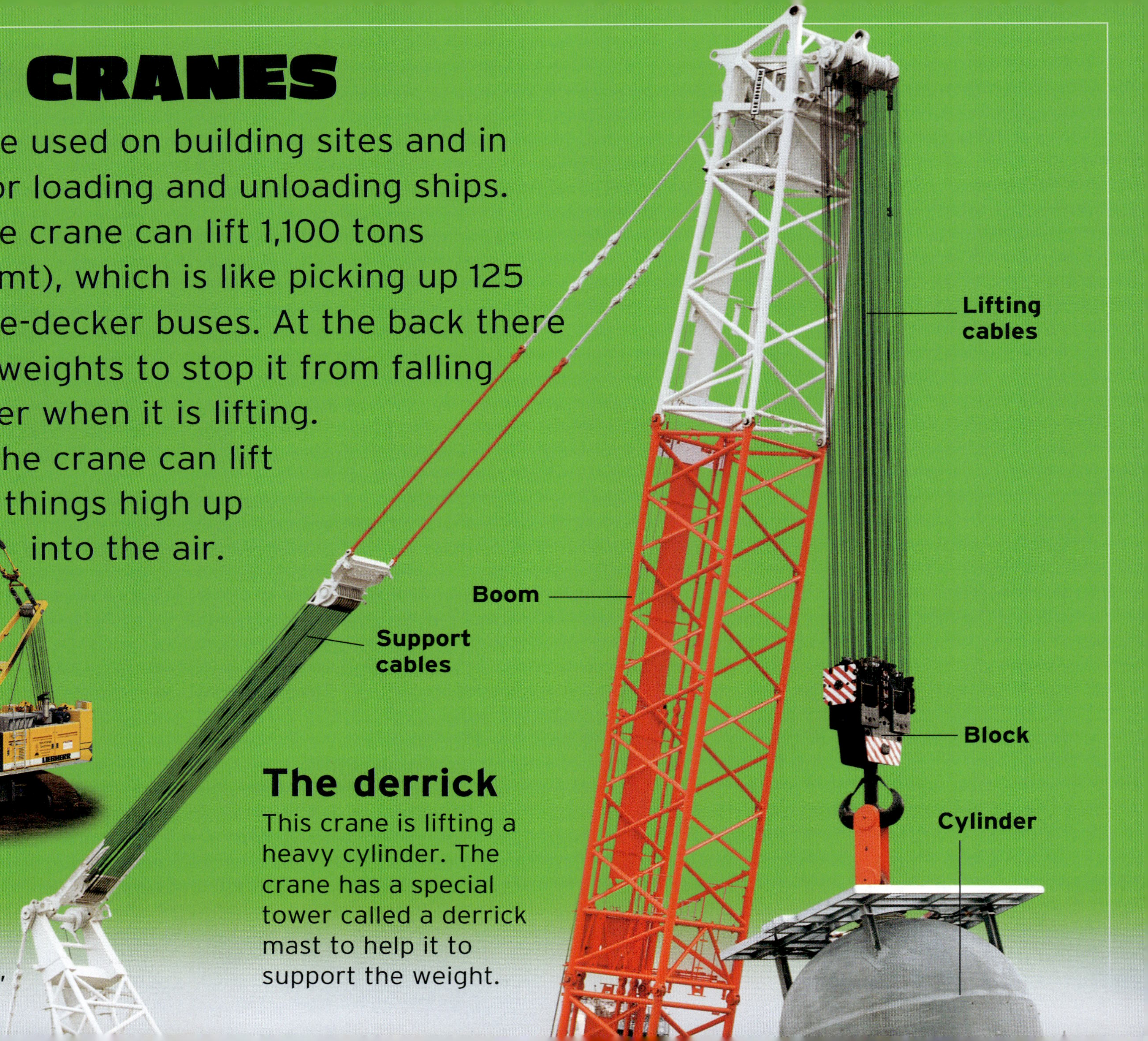

The derrick

This crane is lifting a heavy cylinder. The crane has a special tower called a derrick mast to help it to support the weight.

Derrick mast

GLOSSARY

Asphalt - a black, sticky substance that is mixed with small rocks and becomes hard.

Canopy - something that hangs over a space.

Chevron - a pattern of stripes arranged in a V shape.

Conveyor - a mechanical device used to convey materials from one place to another.

Excavator - a power-driven digging machine.

Exhaust - the smoke or gas given off by an engine.

Jib - the boom (long pole) of a derrick or crane.

Quarry - a large open hole or pit dug for mining stone, gravel, or other matter from the earth.

INDEX